Aurora Gallery

To M[...]
From Dad + M[...]
Purchased in
Leningrad in
July, 1989

The Hermitage

LENINGRAD

WESTERN EUROPEAN PAINTING

AURORA ART PUBLISHERS · LENINGRAD

Introduced by
YURI KUZNETSOV

Translated from the Russian by
VLADIMIR VEZEY

Layout and design by
ILDUS FARRAKHOV

© Aurora Art Publishers, Leningrad, 1988

Printed in Finland

Э $\dfrac{4903020000\text{-}611}{023(01)\text{-}88}$ 52-88

ISBN 5-7300-0101-0

The Picture Gallery constitutes the Hermitage's principal section, as also the oldest in point of time. It came into being with the acquisition, in 1763, of 225 paintings by Western European masters from the Berlin merchant Johann-Ernest Gotzkowsky. Over the next two centuries the Museum's collection increased to 8,000 pictures. Practically all schools and trends that were ever in vogue in Western Europe since the beginnings of easel painting down to the middle of the twentieth century are represented in this collection. The numerous masterpieces on exhibit or in storage have brought the gallery world-wide fame. Every year, more than 3,000,000 visitors from all over the Soviet Union and many foreign countries discover for themselves the celebrated creations of the artistic genius of the peoples of Western Europe.

The first specimens of Western European painting began to reach the shores of the Neva shortly after the founding of the new Russian capital by Peter I. That was a period when Russia's contacts with Western European culture and art had already fallen into a pattern: young Russian artists were perfecting their skill in France and Italy; painters from Germany, France and Switzerland were invited to work in St Petersburg; and the first purchases of canvases were made in Holland and Belgium. In 1716, for instance, 121 pictures were bought for Peter I in Holland by Osip Solovyov and 117 were acquired at the same time in Brussels and Antwerp by a commercial agent named Yuri Kologrivov. Shortly after that the collection was augmented by 119 more canvases sent to Peter I by two English merchants, Evan and Elsen. Predominant in Peter I's collections were Dutch and Flemish paintings. Jacob Stählin, the tsar's biographer, recorded that his favourite artists were Peter Paul Rubens, Anthony Van Dyck, Rembrandt Harmensz van Rijn, Jan Steen, and Adriaen van Ostade, and that his best-liked subjects were genre scenes depicting "Dutch rustics". These Dutch proclivities should not be taken as merely reflecting the personal tastes of Peter "the shipmaster": the burgher democracy of Holland, which had found such vigorous expression in that country's painting, had much in common with the progressive reforms in the field of culture and home life that were being introduced by the tsar in line with the course of national development.

The early part of the eighteenth century saw the establishment of picture galleries in St Petersburg and Peterhof, notably in the Monplaisir Palace which as a court collection may be regarded as the prototype of the Hermitage. The artistic level of these galleries was not all that could be desired, yet some of their exhibits were of outstanding merit and were later added to the "golden

5

fund" of the Hermitage. One such canvas was Rembrandt's *David and Jonathan*, originally exhibited in the Monplaisir and transferred in 1882 to the Hermitage. This, incidentally, was the first Rembrandt to arrive in Russia.

In the mid-eighteenth century the most significant collection of Western European paintings was to be found in the picture hall of the palace in Tsarskoye Selo (now Pushkin). It contained over one hundred canvases, mostly belonging to German, Dutch and Flemish masters, with a sprinkling of French and Italian works, purchased by Georg Grooth, a German painter, at the request of Russian Empress Elizaveta Petrovna. Among these canvases, some of which were even second-rate, there were quite valuable pieces, such as *Danaë* by Jacques Blanchard, *Church Interior* by Emanuel de Witte and *Family Group*, an important work by Daniel Schultz of Danzig (transferred to the Hermitage in 1937).

Many famous Western European collections came to St Petersburg during the reign of Catherine II. Russia, by then, had passsed through two stages of art collecting, which had done much to pave the way for the inauguration of the Hermitage.

While it did contain several first-rate canvases by Rembrandt, Rubens, Frans Hals and Frans Snyders, the Gotzkowsky collection, which formed the original nucleus of the Hermitage, was no different in respect of artistic merit from the purchases made by Peter I and Elizaveta. The acquisition, in 1769, of the collection of Count Heinrich Brühl, a Dresden connoisseur, drastically altered the situation, adding to the Museum's Dutch and Flemish sections works by Rembrandt (including his *Portrait of an Old Man in Red*), Jacob Isaaksz van Ruisdael, Rubens (*Landscape with a Rainbow* and *Perseus and Andromeda*), a series of hunting scenes by Paul de Vos, and several masterpieces of Gerard Ter Borch, Frans Jansz van Mieris I, Adriaen van Ostade, and Philips Wouwerman. There were fewer Italian and French works in the Brühl collection, but it was precisely to it that the Hermitage is indebted for Antoine Watteau's *The Embarrassing Proposal* and *Rest on the Flight into Egypt*, a splendid series of views of Dresden and Pirna copied by Bernardo Bellotto specially for Brühl, and the real gem of his collection: a small-size canvas by Giovanni Battista Tiepolo, known as *Maecenas Presenting the Liberal Arts to Augustus*. This radiant picture had also been painted specially for Brühl (his Dresden palace may be seen in the background) and could be taken as an allusion to the count's activities as a patron of the arts at the court of Augustus III, Elector of Saxony and King of Poland.

In the second half of the eighteenth century, the acquisitions made at the auction sales of private collections in Paris (of J. Aved, J. de Julienne, N. Gaignat, and E.-F. Choiseul), provided the Hermitage with such world-famous masterpieces as *Landscape with Polyphemus* and *Tancred and Erminia* by Nicolas Poussin, *Rest on the Flight into Egypt* and *Boy with a Dog* by Bartolomé Esteban Murillo and Rembrandt's *Return of the Prodigal Son*, his crowning chef-d'oeuvre and one of the supreme creations of man's artistic genius. The monumental, strikingly powerful images of this work reflect the painter's great, all-forgiving love of the people, his faith in their happier future.

A small collection was acquired in 1768 in Brussels from Count Johann-Karl-Philip Cobenzl. Among its best paintings were Rubens's *Roman Charity* (*Cimon and Pero*), *Venus and Adonis* and *Statue of Ceres*. Quite sensational was the purchase in 1772 of 158 canvases belonging to the renowned Parisian collection of Baron Pierre Crozat, which first introduced into Russia the works of the great masters of the Italian Renaissance: Raphael's *Holy Family* (also known as *Madonna and Child with the Beardless St Joseph*), austere and classically pure; Giorgione's *Judith*, shot through with lyric emotion; Titian's *Danaë*, a paean to earthly love; Paolo Veronese's *Pietà*, whose contrasting greens and pinks suggest despairing sorrow; and Tintoretto's thrilling and festive painting, the *Birth of St John the Baptist*.

The works of such eminent seventeenth- and eighteenth-century French artists as Louis Le Nain, Sébastien Bourdon, Nicolas Poussin, Nicolas de Largillière, Antoine Watteau and Jean Baptiste Siméon Chardin laid the beginnings of a special section of French painting. Equally significant and substantial was the increment to the Museum's Dutch and Flemish sections through the acquisition of the Crozat collection. It included a number of priceless canvases – invariably drawing the attention of experts and connoisseurs – such as Rembrandt's *Danaë*, Rubens's *Bacchus*, *Portrait of a Lady-in-Waiting to the Infanta Isabella* and a set of sketches for the *Life of Maria de' Medici* cycle, as well as Van Dyck's *Self-Portrait*.

No less important was the Museum's acquisition of Sir Robert Walpole's collection (Houghton Hall picture gallery) in London in 1779. This added to the Flemish section more works by Rubens (*The Carters*, *Feast in the House of Simon*, sketches for triumphal arches and for the ceiling of the Banqueting House at Whitehall), several Van Dycks, among others *Rest on the Flight into Egypt* (*Madonna of the Partridges*), a series of Frans Snyders's monumental *Shops,* and pictures by Jacob Jordaens and David Teniers the Younger. The works of such prominent seventeenth-century artists as Guido Reni, Francesco Albani, Carlo Maratti, Francesco de Rosa and Luca Giordano enriched the Mu-

7

seum's section of Italian art while its Rembrandt collection was augmented by one of the master's earlier canvases, *The Sacrifice of Isaac.*

Although it is difficult to name the most valuable works of the Walpole collection, it would perhaps be proper to state that Rubens's sketches for the triumphal arches erected to solemnize the arrival of Cardinal Infante Ferdinand in Antwerp, and for the ceiling of the Banqueting House at Whitehall, were among its most interesting holdings. These lightning sketches reveal a new Rubens, not the fashionable "painter of royalty" but an artist anxious to seize in his daily work the fortunate flashes of inspiration that visited him and to record the images evoked. Together with those of the *Life of Maria de' Medici* cycle, they constitute the world's best collection of Rubens's sketches.

The last addition of any importance to the Hermitage stocks during the eighteenth century came with the purchase, in 1781, of the Baudouin collection in Paris. It comprised 119 canvases, including those by Rembrandt, Van Dyck, van Ostade and Jacob Isaaksz van Ruisdael.

A momentous event in the history of the Hermitage picture gallery in the late eighteenth century was the acquisition of works by contemporary artists. These were Anton Raphael Mengs and Angelica Kauffmann of Germany, Pompeo Batoni of Italy, Joseph Wright of England, and Jean-Baptiste Greuze of France, all associated with the newest movements of Classicism and Sentimentalism. Apart from that, a number of leading contemporary artists were doing work expressly for Russia. Thus, Joshua Reynolds was busy with his vast canvas *The Infant Hercules Strangling the Serpents Sent by Hera*, François Boucher painted the decorative panel *Pygmalion and Galatea* and Jean Baptiste Siméon Chardin executed his *Still Life with the Attributes of the Arts*. These pieces were closely connected with the history and culture of Russia: Reynolds's picture was symbolic of Russia's successful début in the international arena, while the works of Boucher and Chardin were intended for the Academy of Arts just established in St Petersburg.

The exceptionally high quality of the paintings acquired by the Museum towards the close of the eighteenth century should be attributed to the calibre of the men in charge of purchases, enlightened Russians, notably Dmitry Golitsyn, Russian ambassador to Paris and The Hague, and also to the cooperation of highly competent foreign experts, such as Melchior Grimm, Dénis Diderot, François Tronchin and Etienne-Maurice Falconet. A manuscript catalogue of the picture gallery compiled in 1797 listed 3,996 pictures, including numerous masterpieces.

Acquisitions continued during the nineteenth century, though at a slower pace. In 1814 and 1815, seventy-five canvases were bought in Amsterdam from the English banker Coesvelt, among them the *Portrait of Count-Duke of Olivares*, a brilliant example of the realistic art of the great Velázquez. This acquisition laid the corner-stone of the Museum's section of Spanish paintings, which was soon augmented by the purchase at an auction in Paris, in 1831, of the collection of Manuel de Godoy, a former minister of Charles IV of Spain, and by canvases bought in 1834 from Paez de la Cadeña, Spanish ambassador to Russia.

After the end of the Patriotic War of 1812 Alexander I acquired 118 canvases from the Malmaison palace of the Empress Josephine, the first wife of Napoleon. Composed mainly of the spoils of the Napoleonic wars, this collection contained several outstanding works of the Dutch school (Rembrandt's *Descent from the Cross*, Paulus Potter's *Farm*, Ter Borch's *Glass of Lemonade*), the Flemish school (Rubens's *Descent from the Cross*, Tenier's *Apes in the Kitchen*), and the French school (*Times of Day* series by Claude Gellée called Lorrain).

In the first half of the nineteenth century the Museum came into possession of such chefs-d'oeuvre of late sixteenth-century Italian painting as Caravaggio's *The Lute Player* and Annibale Carracci's *The Three Maries at the Sepulchre*, which meant that the two masters were now represented in the Hermitage by the finest specimens of their art.

A milestone in the history of the Hermitage was reached when, in the middle of the nineteenth century, the Museum acquired the collection of the Barbarigo Palace in Venice, which provided it with most of its Titians, and the collections of Marshal Soult in Paris and Willem II of the Netherlands. The latter collection was of particular value since it included the works of Rogier van der Weyden, Jan Gossaert (also known as Mabuse) and Jan Provost – early painters of the Netherlands hitherto unrepresented in the Museum.

In 1852 the Hermitage picture gallery moved into the New Hermitage building (designed by Leo von Klenze) and was thrown open to the public. In addition to Western European paintings, it boasted the best works of the Russian school, which, however, were transferred in 1898 to the Alexander III Museum (now the Russian Museum). The Hermitage, meanwhile, continued to be the property of the Imperial family in the charge of the Ministry of the Court. New acquisitions were made with great difficulty, a special authorization being needed in each particular case. In 1865 the Museum acquired from the Duke of Litta, in Milan, Leonardo da Vinci's *Madonna and Child*, the first canvas of the great master to reach Russia; and in 1870 it bought Raphael's *Madonna and*

Child, a lyrical canvas with a pellucid spring landscape owned by Count Conestabile of Perugia.

In the 1880s purchases abroad were all but discontinued, though it was just at this time that the Hermitage received seventy-three of the best pictures of the Golitsyn Museum in Moscow, among them *The Annunciation* by Cima da Conegliano and a *Townscape* by Francesco Guardi.

Important acquisitions were resumed only in the early twentieth century, with the purchase, in 1910, of the collection of Piotr Semionov-Tien-Shansky and, in 1914, of Leonardo da Vinci's *Madonna with a Flower* (*The Benois Madonna*). In 1911 a number of rare works of the Italian trecento and quattrocento entered the Museum, notably Simone Martini's *Madonna of the Annunciation*, the reliquary with the representation of Christ and angels by Fra Beato Angelico from Grigory Stroganov's Roman collection and Filippino Lippi's *Adoration of the Infant Christ* from Paul Stroganov's St Petersburg collection. In 1915 and 1916 the Hermitage came into possession of the V.P. Zurov and A.Z. Khitrovo bequests.

These last pre-revolutionary accretions to the Hermitage picture gallery were exceptionally valuable. The collection of the celebrated Russian scholar and traveller Semionov-Tien-Shansky, which numbered more than 700 canvases, made the Museum's Dutch section one of the richest in the world and gave the gallery over 400 works of Minor Dutchmen that had hitherto been practically or entirely unrepresented.

The Khitrovo bequest enabled the Museum to establish an excellent exhibition of English painting at the peak of its development: the works of Thomas Gainsborough, Henry Raeburn, George Romney, John Hoppner, John Opie and Thomas Lawrence.

After the 1917 Revolution the Hermitage entered a new phase of its history. Lenin's decrees on the nationalization and preservation of art treasures made it possible to undertake a systematic enrichment of the country's museums with works of art.

The famous collections of Russian noblemen, such as the Stroganovs, Sheremetevs, Shuvalovs, and Yusupovs, were initially turned into public museums, but later transferred, either wholly or partially, to the Hermitage. Significant additions followed the nationalization of the private collections of Argutinsky-Dolgorukov, the Vorontsov-Dashkovs, Gorchakovs, Miatlevs and Olives.

The materials of the former Museum of Christian Relics at the Academy of Arts and of Nikolai Likhachov's collection served to enrich the section of Italian art and to increase its attraction. The works of Ugolino Lorenzetti, Spinello Aretino, Fra Filippo Lippi, Lorenzo Costa, Francesco Francia, and other masters enabled the Museum to unfold an exhibition of trecento and quattrocento art. The canvases of Bartolommeo Manfredi, Mattia Preti, Bernardo Strozzi, Luca Giordano and certain other exponents of the realistic trend did much to round out the exhibition of seventeenth-century Italian art, while that of the eighteenth century gained very substantially through the transfer – from the Museum of the Stieglitz School of Art and Industrial Design – of Giovanni Battista Tiepolo's monumental canvases on subjects from Roman history and of Francesco Guardi's superb *Landscape* from the Gatchina Palace. The Italian section, embracing the period from the thirteenth to the eighteenth century, now totalled more than 1,000 canvases. Today it is unquestionably one of the best collections outside Italy, though not all the schools of Italian art are illustrated in it as fully as that of sixteenth – eighteenth-century Venice. There are essential gaps, as, for example, in the case of Florence, Rome, Padua and of some other cities. On the whole, seventeenth- and eighteenth-century Italian painting is represented considerably better than the art of earlier periods.

The nationalization of private collections benefited the section of French painting, which acquired for the first time a number of works by fifteenth- and sixteenth-century French masters, while the collection of seventeenth- and eighteenth-century French artists, finally completed in the early post-revolutionary years, became the next best and richest after that of the Louvre.

Among the most valuable acquisitions was the *Entry into Jerusalem* by an anonymous fifteenth-century artist, illustrative of the beginnings of easel painting in France, as well as *St Sebastian before Diocletian and Maximian*, presumably executed by Josse Lieferinxe, who worked in the late fifteenth century.

A definitely fuller interpretation of seventeenth-century French realistic art became possible with the acquisition of Pierre Montallier's *Acts of Mercy* (the only authentic work of this follower of the brothers Le Nain), and a *Self-Portrait* by Jean Daret. Most of the new accessions, however, served to augment the Museum's collection of eighteenth-century French paintings, the works of the leading masters of that period being of exceptionally high quality. These included Watteau's *Capricious Girl*, Lemoyne's *Virgin*, Boucher's *Triumph of Venus*, Greuze's *Spoilt Child* and several portraits, Fragonard's *The Lost Forfeit*, Hubert Robert's *Villa Madama near Rome* and *Ruins of a Terrace in a Park*. In 1926 the Museum regained possession of Chardin's best still life, known as *Still Life with the Attributes of the Arts*, which had been sold in 1854 by order of Nicholas I.

11

The collection of French painting of the period from the fifteenth to eighteenth centuries now totals over 600 canvases.

Quite a few important works have been added to the Netherlandish, Flemish and Dutch sections. In the Flemish section special mention should be made of *Christ Crowned with Thorns*, *Susanna and the Elders* and the sketch *Descent from the Cross* by Rubens, three portraits by Van Dyck, and Jordaens's canvas *The Bean King*, which reveals with particular brilliance and candour the democratic, popular roots of Flemish art. The Museum's Flemish section now houses nearly 600 pictures.

The gallery possesses three canvases of Abraham Bloemaert, who trained a brilliant galaxy of Utrecht painters. The collection of works by the Utrecht Caravaggists has been augmented through the acquisition from the Argutinsky-Dolgorukov gallery of Hendrick Terbrugghen's *Concert*, the master's only work owned by the Hermitage, and through the purchase from Piotr Durnovo of the *Childhood of Christ*, regarded as one of the best canvases by Gerard van Honthorst. There have been further accessions to the exhibition of the Haarlem academic painters, such as the *Massacre of the Innocents* by Karel van Mander, which came in 1921 from the collection of Nikolai Roerich, Russian artist of note, and the *Sinners before the Flood* by Cornelis Cornelisz. van Haarlem, received somewhat later from the Pavlovsk Palace.

One of Rembrandt's very rare grisailles, the *Adoration of the Magi*, was added to the magnificent collection of his works at the Hermitage. Acquired in 1923, it was only recently attributed to the master.

The Museum's collection of Dutch paintings of the so-called Golden Age – portraiture, genre and still life – has become one of the largest in the world, totalling over 1,300 exhibits.

Some very interesting and important accessions have increased the collections of German, Spanish and English painting. The Spanish section, for instance, has obtained a *Crucifixion* by Francisco de Zurbarán and an *Annunciation* by José Claudio Antolinez, and the English section – Wright's *The Annual Girandola: Castel Sant' Angelo in Rome* and Morland's *Approaching Storm*.

The works of Danish, Swedish, Norwegian and Finnish artists, acquired from various palace galleries and private individuals, formed the nucleus of a modest section of Scandinavian art.

The most important result of the Museum's efforts in the field of collecting after 1917 has been the creation of a section of modern and contemporary art. It was based on the collection of the Kushelev Gallery at the Academy of Arts, transferred to the Hermitage in 1922. The Gallery of Count Nikolai Kushelev-Bezborodko, bequeathed by him to the Academy, was represented mainly by French, Dutch and German artists active during the first half of the nineteenth century. This acquisition gave the Hermitage its first works of Eugène Delacroix and Hippolyte Delaroche of the romantic school; Théodore Rousseau, Charles François Daubigny and Jules Dupré of the Barbizon school, and painters closely associated with it, such as Narcisse Virgile Díaz de la Peña, Charles Emile Jacque, Constant Troyon, and Jean Baptiste Camille Corot; and, finally, Gustave Courbet and Jean François Millet, regarded as the leading exponents of the realistic and democratic trend of the nineteenth century. Works by their contemporaries were received at the same time, including those of Ferdinand de Braeckelaer, Louis Gallait, Nicaise de Keyser, and Hendrick Leys of Belgium, Jan Weissenbruch, Willem Roelofs and Petrus van Schendel of Holland, and the Achenbach brothers and Ludwig Knaus of Germany.

In 1929 the Museum's section of nineteenth-century art was augmented by canvases collected by the Russian landscape painter Alexei Bogoliubov for the Anichkov Palace. Of very great importance for the Museum's picture gallery were a number of French paintings of the classical school. These came in the 1920s from the Yusupov and Naryshkina collections and included *Sappho and Phaon* by Jacques Louis David, *Morpheus and Iris* by Pierre-Narcisse Guérin, *Innocence Preferring Love to Wealth* by Pierre Paul Prud'hon and *Portrait of Count Nikolai Guryev* by Dominique Ingres.

In 1930 and 1931, following the redistribution of art treasures among the museums of Moscow and Leningrad, the Hermitage received numerous works by Claude Monet, Auguste Renoir, Paul Cézanne, Vincent Van Gogh, Paul Gauguin, Pablo Picasso, Henri Matisse, Albert Marquet, and other artists of the late nineteenth and early twentieth centuries. All these canvases were purchased in former times by the Moscow collectors Sergei Shchukin and Ivan Morozov. Shchukin started collecting the Impressionists and Postimpressionists in the 1890s. Subsequently he took keen interest in Picasso and Matisse and their works composed two-thirds of his collection. The highly representative Morozov collection took shape between 1904 and 1914 and reflected its owner's keen judgment and unerring taste.

The first batch of modern paintings was soon followed by a second, as a result of the closing, in 1948, of the Museum of Modern Western Art, which had retained the bulk of the Shchukin and Morozov collections, and the sharing of its treasures between the Pushkin Museum of Fine Arts in Moscow and the Hermitage.

At present the Hermitage collection of French paintings of the late nineteenth and early twentieth centuries numbers over 280 canvases, including eight Monets, six Renoirs, two Pissarros, three Sisleys, and six Degas pastels. The Postimpressionist section has fifteen Gauguins, eleven Cézannes and four Van Goghs. Even more impressive is the exhibition of the following generation of artists, which contains thirty-seven Matisses, nine Marquets, fourteen Derains, nine Bonnards, twenty-one Denis, and over thirty Picassos.

By comparison with this collection, which is one of the world's greatest, the Museum's exhibition of works belonging to other national schools of painting of the late nineteenth and early twentieth centuries is more modest. The German school is something of an exception, being rather well illustrated by the works of Wilhelm Leibl, Franz Stuck, Heinrich Campendonk, Heinrich Ehmsen, Otto Nagel and Hans Grundig, even though in some cases by single canvases.

The latest section of the picture gallery is that of the socialist countries of Europe. The task of expanding this section is currently being given top priority by the Museum.

During the past few years the Museum's collections have been augmented by acquisitions made by its Expert-Purchasing Commission and by gifts received from artists or members of their families and from collectors. In this way the Hermitage has come into possession of such canvases as Jacques Bellange's *Lamentation*, Massimo Stanzione's *Cleopatra*, Adriaen van Ostade's *Rustic Society*, Nicolaes Berchem's *Pastoral Scene*, Eugène Boudin's *Beach*, Renato Guttuso's *Crowd*, *Rocco and His Son* and still life *Potatoes on Yellow Paper*, André Fougeron's *Chad-Fishers* and *Bridge*, etc.

In terms of completeness and selection the Hermitage collection of Western European painting is one of the best in the world. It embraces all national schools and the work of many celebrated masters. Its exhibits offer an excellent opportunity for studying Western European painting of the thirteenth to the twentieth century and for assessing the contribution of each school and epoch to the development of art the world over. A visit to the Hermitage picture gallery provides an aesthetic experience of a very high order.

Yuri Kuznetsov

PLATES

SIMONE MARTINI
ANONYMOUS ARTIST OF
THE 15TH CENTURY
FRA GIOVANNI DA FIESOLE
ANGELICO
PIETRO PERUGINO
FILIPPINO LIPPI
LEONARDO DA VINCI
RAPHAEL
GIORGIONE
ROBERT CAMPIN
ROGIER VAN DER WEYDEN
PIETER BRUEGHEL THE YOUNGER
MASTER OF THE FEMALE
HALF-LENGTHS
ANONYMOUS ARTIST OF
THE 16TH CENTURY
CORREGGIO
TITIAN
PARMIGIANINO
VERONESE
TINTORETTO
LUIS DE MORALES
EL GRECO
JUAN PANTOJA DE LA CRUZ
JUAN BAUTISTA DEL MAINO
DIEGO DE SILVA VELÁZQUEZ
FRANCISCO DE ZURBARÁN
CARAVAGGIO
ANNIBALE CARRACCI
JOSÉ DE RIBERA
ANTONIO DE PEREDA
BARTOLOMÉ ESTEBAN MURILLO
FRANCISCO JOSÉ DE GOYA Y
LUCIENTES
HANS WERTINGER
LUCAS CRANACH THE ELDER
GEORG FLEGEL
CHRISTOPH PAUDISS
ABRAHAM BLOEMAERT
PAULUS MOREELSE
GERRIT VAN HONTHORST
JAN VAN GOYEN
FRANS HALS
REMBRANDT HARMENSZ VAN RIJN
ADRIAEN VAN OSTADE
LUDOLF BAKHUIJZEN
PIETER CLAESZ
PIETER DE HOOCH
WILLEM KALF
GABRIEL METSU
JAN STEEN

JAN BRUEGHEL
('VELVET' BRUEGHEL)
JACOB JORDAENS
GIJSBRECHTS LIJTENS
FRANS SNYDERS
PETER PAUL RUBENS
ANTHONY VAN DYCK
JAN FYT
BERNARDO STROZZI
GUIDO RENI
MICHELANGELO DA CAMPIDOGLIO
MATTIA PRETI
LUCA GIORDANO
NICOLAS POUSSIN
CLAUDE GELLÉE
(CLAUDE LORRAIN)
LOUIS LE NAIN
PETER LELY
THOMAS GAINSBOROUGH
JOSHUA REYNOLDS
GEORGE MORLAND
CANALETTO
FRANCESCO GUARDI
GIOVANNI BATTISTA TIEPOLO
JEAN-MARC NATTIER
ANTOINE WATTEAU
FRANÇOIS BOUCHER
JEAN BAPTISTE SIMÉON CHARDIN
HUBERT ROBERT
JEAN HONORÉ FRAGONARD
CASPAR DAVID FRIEDRICH
ANTON RAFFAEL MENGS
JEAN FRANÇOIS MILLET
EUGÈNE DELACROIX
HORACE VERNET
THÉODORE ROUSSEAU
CONSTANT TROYON
CHARLES FRANÇOIS DAUBIGNY
CLAUDE OSCAR MONET
PIERRE AUGUSTE RENOIR
ALFRED SISLEY
CAMILLE PISSARRO
VINCENT VAN GOGH
PAUL GAUGUIN
HENRI MATISSE
MAURICE DENIS
MAURICE DE VLAMINCK
PAUL CÉZANNE
HENRI ROUSSEAU
KEES VAN DONGEN
PABLO PICASSO
RENATO GUTTUSO

1. SIMONE MARTINI. *Ca.* 1284–1344. *Italy*

Madonna of the Annunciation. Wing of a diptych.
Second half, 1330s

Tempera on panel. 30.5 × 21.5*

---

* All measurements are in centimetres.

2. ANONYMOUS ARTIST OF THE 15TH CENTURY
(MASTER OF THE THUISON ALTARPIECE). *France*

The Entry into Jerusalem. Wing of an altarpiece

Oil on panel. 116.5 × 51.5

3. FRA GIOVANNI DA FIESOLE ANGELICO
(called FRA BEATO). *Ca.* 1400–1455. *Italy*

**Madonna and Child with St Dominic and St Thomas
Aquinas.** *Ca.* 1430

Fresco. 196 × 187

4. PIETRO PERUGINO (PIETRO VANNUCCI).
Ca. 1450–1523. *Italy*

Portrait of a Young Man. Mid-1490s

Oil on canvas, transferred from a panel. 40.5 × 25.5

5. FILIPPINO LIPPI. *Ca.* 1457–1504. *Italy*

The Adoration of the Infant Christ. 1480s

Oil on copperplate, transferred from a panel. Tondo, diam. 53

6. LEONARDO DA VINCI. 1452–1519. *Italy*

Madonna with a Flower (The Benois Madonna).
Begun 1478

Oil on canvas, transferred from a panel. 49.5 × 31.5

7. RAPHAEL (RAFFAELLO SANTI). 1483–1520. *Italy*

Madonna and Child (The Conestabile Madonna).
Late 1502 – early 1503

Tempera on canvas, transferred from a panel. 17.5 × 18

8. GIORGIONE (GIORGIO DA CASTELFRANCO).
Ca. 1478–1510. *Italy*

Judith

Oil on canvas, transferred from a panel. 144 × 66.5

9. ROBERT CAMPIN. *Ca.* 1380–1444. *The Netherlands*

Virgin and Child at the Fireside. Right wing of a diptych

Oil on panel. 34.3 × 24.5

10. ROGIER VAN DER WEYDEN.
Ca. 1400–1464. *The Netherlands*

**St Luke Drawing a Portrait
of the Virgin**

Oil on canvas, transferred from a panel. 102.5 × 108.5

11. PIETER BRUEGHEL THE YOUNGER.
Ca. 1564–1638. *The Netherlands*

The Adoration of the Magi

Signed, bottom left: *P. Brueghel*
Oil on canvas, transferred
from a panel. 36 × 56

12. MASTER OF THE FEMALE HALF-LENGTHS.
Active first half of the 16th century. *The Netherlands*

Virgin and Child

Oil on panel. 53.2 × 42.5

13. ANONYMOUS ARTIST OF THE 16TH CENTURY.
France

Portrait of an Unknown Man. Late 1560s

Inscribed at a later date, top right: *M: Le Duc D'alençon*
Oil on panel. 48.5 × 32

14. CORREGGIO (ANTONIO ALLEGRI). 1489–1534.
Italy

Portrait of a Lady

Signed, left, on the tree: *ANTON LAET*
Oil on canvas. 103 × 87

15. TITIAN (TIZIANO VECELLIO). 1485/90–1576. *Italy*
Portrait of a Young Woman. 1530s

Oil on canvas. 96 × 75

16. TITIAN
(TIZIANO VECELLIO).
1485/90–1576. *Italy*

Danaë.
Between 1546 and 1553

Oil on canvas. 120 × 187

17. PARMIGIANINO (FRANCESCO MAZZOLA).
1503–1540. *Italy*

The Entombment. *Ca.* 1523

Oil on canvas, transferred from a panel. 39 7/8 x 26 5/8

→

18. VERONESE (PAOLO CALIARI).
1528–1588. *Italy*

The Adoration of the Magi. Early 1570s

Oil on copperplate. 45 × 34.5

19. TINTORETTO (JACOPO ROBUSTI).
1518–1594. *Italy*

The Birth of St John the Baptist. 1550s

Oil on canvas. 181 × 266

20. LUIS DE MORALES. 1510–1586. *Spain*

Madonna and Child with a Cross-shaped Distaff

Oil on canvas, transferred from a panel. 71.5 × 52

21. EL GRECO (DOMENIKOS THEOTOKOPOULOS).
1541–1614. *Spain*

St Peter and St Paul. Between 1587 and 1592

Half-obliterated signature, bottom right: *Domenikos Theotokopoulos epoiei*
Oil on canvas. 121.5 × 105

22. JUAN PANTOJA DE LA CRUZ. 1553–1608. *Spain*

Portrait of Diego de Villamayor. 1605

Signed and dated, bottom right: *Ju... es Pantoja de la + Faciebat 1605*
Inscribed in abbreviated Latin form, top background: *Didac [us de Villamaiore]*.
Ætatis suæ (left), 17. ANNO. 1605 (right)
Oil on canvas. 89 × 71

23. JUAN BAUTISTA DEL MAINO. 1578–1649. *Spain*

The Adoration of the Shepherds

Signed, right, on the remains of a column: *F. IV̊. BTA*
Oil on canvas. 143.5 × 100.5

24. DIEGO DE SILVA VELÁZQUEZ. 1599–1660. *Spain*
Luncheon. *Ca.* 1617–18

Oil on canvas. 107.5 × 102

25. FRANCISCO DE ZURBARÁN. 1598–1664. *Spain*

The Girlhood of the Virgin. *Ca.* 1660

Oil on canvas. 73.5 × 53.5

26. CARAVAGGIO
(MICHELANGELO MERISI DA
CARAVAGGIO). 1571–1610. *Italy*

The Lute Player. Ca. 1595

Oil on canvas. 94 x 119

27. ANNIBALE CARRACCI. 1560–1609. *Italy*

The Three Maries at the Sepulchre. Second half, 1590s

Oil on canvas. 121 × 145.5

28. JOSÉ DE RIBERA. 1591–1652. *Spain*

Allegory of History

Signed with initials, bottom right; inscribed on the spine of the book:
Thucydides
Oil on canvas. 113 × 81

29. ANTONIO DE PEREDA.
Ca. 1608–1678. *Spain*
Still Life. *Ca.* 1652

Signed, middle, on one of the drawers: *Pereda f*
Oil on canvas. 80 × 94

30. BARTOLOMÉ ESTEBAN MURILLO. 1617–1682.
Spain

The Holy Family. *Ca.* 1665

Oil on panel. 23.8 × 18

31. FRANCISCO JOSÉ DE GOYA Y LUCIENTES.
1746–1828. *Spain*

Portrait of Antonia Zárate. *Ca.* 1811

Oil on canvas. 71 × 58

32. HANS WERTINGER (called SCHWAB).
Ca. 1465/70–1533. *Germany*

Rural Fête (October)

Oil on panel. 22.5 × 40

33. LUCAS CRANACH THE ELDER. 1472–1553.
Germany

The Virgin and Child under the Apple-tree

Signed with the winged dragon, right, on the trunk
Oil on canvas, transferred from a panel. 87 × 59

34. GEORG FLEGEL. 1566–1638. *Germany*

Still Life with Flowers and Food

Monogrammed, right on the table: *GF*
Oil on canvas. 52.5 × 41

35. CHRISTOPH PAUDISS. *Ca.* 1618–1666. *Germany*
Still Life. 1660

Signed and dated, on the edge of the table: *Cristoffer Paudiß. 1660*
Oil on canvas, transferred from a panel. 62 × 46.5

36. ABRAHAM BLOEMAERT. 1564–1651. *Holland*

Landscape with Tobias and the Angel

Oil on canvas. 139 × 107.5

37. PAULUS MOREELSE. 1571–1638. *Holland*

Portrait of a Young Woman with a String of Pearls

Oil on panel. 67.5 × 52.5 (oval)

→

39. JAN VAN GOYEN. 1596–1656. *Holland*

The Skaters. 1641

Signed and dated, bottom left: *v Goyen 1641*
Oil on panel. 32 × 55

38. GERRIT VAN HONTHORST. 1590–1656. *Holland*

The Childhood of Christ. *Ca.* 1620

Oil on canvas. 137.5 × 185

40. FRANS HALS. 1581/85–1666. *Holland*

Portrait of a Man. Before 1660

Monogrammed, right, on the background: *FH*
Oil on canvas. 84.5 × 67

41. REMBRANDT HARMENSZ VAN RIJN. 1606–1669.
Holland

The Holy Family with Angels. 1645

Signed and dated, bottom left: *Rembrandt f. 1645*
Oil on canvas. 117 × 91

42. REMBRANDT HARMENSZ VAN RIJN. 1606–1669.
Holland

Portrait of an Old Man in Red. *Ca.* 1652–54

Oil on canvas. 108 × 86

43. ADRIAEN VAN OSTADE. 1610–1685. *Holland*

Village Musicians. 1645

Signed and dated, bottom right: *Av. OS[..] de 16 [.] 5*
Oil on panel. 39 × 30.5

44. LUDOLF BAKHUIJZEN.
1631–1708. *Holland*

Shipwreck by the Coastal Cliffs

Oil on canvas. 52.5 X 68

45. PIETER CLAESZ.
1596/97–1661. *Holland*

Still Life with Ham. 1647

Monogrammed and dated, left: *16 PC 47*
Oil on panel. 40 × 61

46. PIETER DE HOOCH. 1629–after 1684. *Holland*

Mistress and Maid. *Ca.* 1660

Oil on canvas. 53 × 42

47. WILLEM KALF. 1619–1693. *Holland*

Dessert

Signed, bottom left: *W. Kalf*
Oil on canvas. 105 × 87.5

48. GABRIEL METSU. 1629–1667. *Holland*

Treating to Oysters. *Ca.* 1660

Signed, top left: *G Metsu*
Oil on panel. 56 × 42

49. JAN STEEN. 1625/26–1679. *Holland*

Backgammon Players. 1667

Signed and dated in the cartouche, above the door: *J. Steen. 1667*
Oil on panel. 45.5 × 39

50. JAN BRUEGHEL
('VELVET' BRUEGHEL).
1568–1625. *Flanders*

Village Street

Oil on copperplate. 25.5 × 38

51. JACOB JORDAENS.
1593–1678. *Flanders*

The Bean King. *Ca.* 1638

Oil on canvas. 157 × 211

52. GIJSBRECHTS LIJTENS. 1586–after 1643. *Flanders*

Winter Landscape

Oil on panel. 71.5 × 89

53. FRANS SNYDERS. 1579–1657. *Flanders*

Still Life with Dead Game and Lobster

Oil on canvas. 121 × 181

54. PETER PAUL RUBENS.
1577–1640. *Flanders*

Landscape with a Rainbow
Between 1632 and 1635

Oil on canvas, transferred
from a panel. 86 × 130

55. PETER PAUL RUBENS. 1577–1640. *Flanders*

The Union of Earth and Water. *Ca* 1618

Oil on canvas. 222.5 × 180.5

56. ANTHONY VAN DYCK. 1599–1641. *Flanders*
Family Group. 1621

Oil on canvas. 113.5 × 93.5

57. JAN FYT. 1611–1661. *Flanders*

Still Life with Flowers,
Fruit and Parrot

Signed, left, on the stone. *Joannes Fyt*
Oil on canvas. 134 × 171

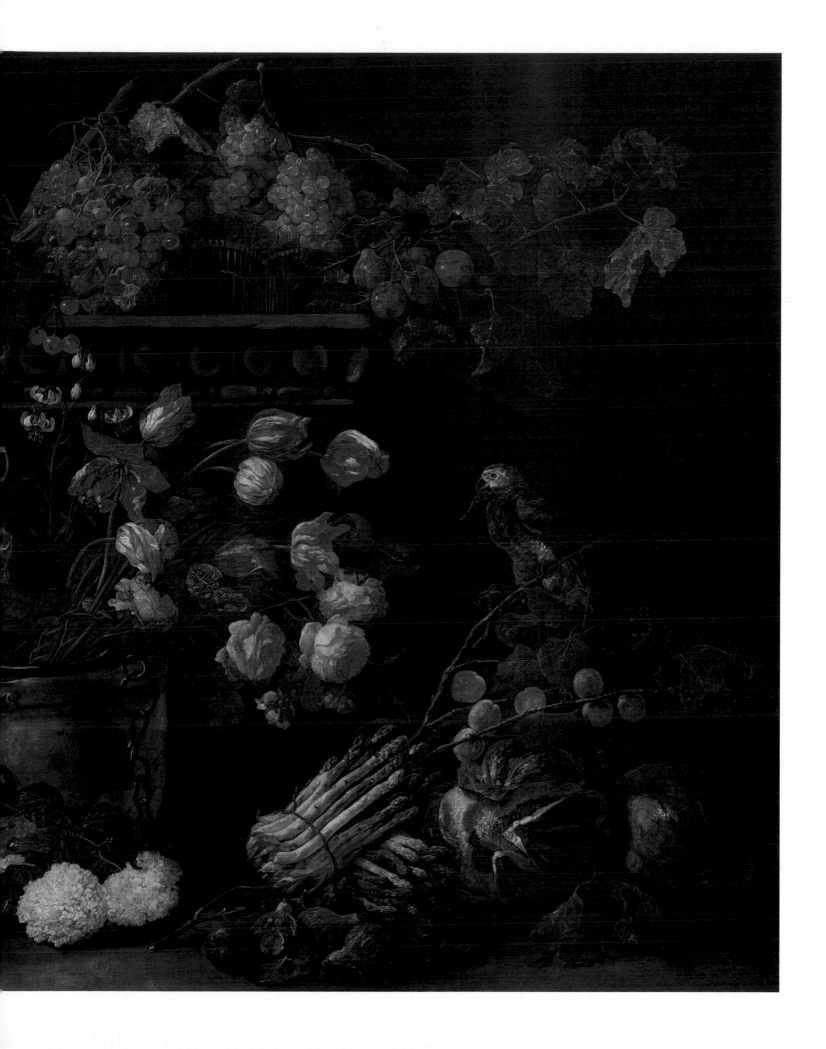

58. ANTHONY VAN DYCK. 1599–1641. *Flanders*

**Portrait of Anne Dalkeith, Countess Morton (?),
and Anne Kirke.** 1630s

Oil on canvas. 131.5 × 150.6

59. BERNARDO STROZZI. 1581–1644. *Italy*
The Healing of Tobit. *Ca.* 1635

Oil on canvas. 158 × 223.5

80. GUIDO RENI. 1575–1642. *Italy*
The Rape of Europa. *Ca.* 1609

Oil on canvas. 114 × 88.5

61. MICHELANGELO DA CAMPIDOGLIO
(MICHELANGELO DI PACE). 1610–1670. *Italy*

Still Life with Grapes

Oil on canvas. 98 × 134

62. MATTIA PRETI. 1613–1699. *Italy*
Musical Party. 1630s

Oil on canvas. 110 × 117

63. LUCA GIORDANO. 1632–1705. *Italy*

The Forge of Vulcan

Oil on canvas, transferred from a panel. 192.5 × 151.5

64. NICOLAS POUSSIN. 1594–1665.
France
Tancred and Erminia. 1630s

Oil on canvas. 98.6 × 146.5

65. CLAUDE GELLÉE (CLAUDE LORRAIN).
1600–1682. *France*

Morning in the Harbour. 1640s

Jan Miel of Flanders (1599–1663) is thought to have painted
the figures

Oil on canvas. 74×97

66. LOUIS LE NAIN. *Ca.* 1593–1648. *France*
The Milkwoman's Family. 1640s

Oil on canvas. 51 × 59

67. PETER LELY (PIETER VAN DER FAES).
1618–1680. *England*
Portrait of Cecilia Croft (Killigrew)
Oil on canvas. 70 × 55,5 (oval)

68. THOMAS GAINSBOROUGH. 1727–1788. *England*
Lady in Blue. 1770s

Oil on canvas. 76 × 64

69. JOSHUA REYNOLDS. 1723–1792. *England*

Cupid Untying the Zone of Venus. *Ca.* 1788

Oil on canvas. 127.5 × 101

70. GEORGE MORLAND. 1763–1804. *England*

An Approaching Storm. 1791

Signed and dated, right, on the cut of a trunk: *G. Morland, 1791*
Oil on canvas. 85 × 117

71. CANALETTO (ANTONIO
CANALE). 1697–1768. *Italy*

**The Arrival of the French Ambassador
in Venice**

Oil on canvas. 181 × 259.5

72. FRANCESCO GUARDI. 1712–1793. *Italy*

View of a Square with Palace

Oil on panel. 27 x 23

73. GIOVANNI BATTISTA TIEPOLO. 1696–1770. *Italy*

**Maecenas Presenting the Liberal Arts
to Augustus.** *Ca.* 1745

Oil on canvas. 69.5 × 89

74. JEAN-MARC NATTIER. 1685–1766. *France*

Portrait of a Lady in Grey

Signed, left, near the shoulder: *Nattier pinxit*
Oil on canvas. 80 X 64 (oval)

75. ANTOINE WATTEAU. 1684–1721. *France*

Savoyard with a Marmot. 1716

Oil on canvas. 40.5 × 32.5

76. FRANÇOIS BOUCHER.
1703–1770, *France*

Landscape near Beauvais. Early 1740s

Signed, bottom right: *f. Boucher*

Oil on canvas 19 1 (50

77. JEAN BAPTISTE SIMÉON CHARDIN. 1699–1779. *France*

Still Life with the Attributes of the Arts. 1766

Signed and dated, bottom left, on the edge of the table: *CHARDIN 1766*

Oil on canvas. 112 × 140.5

78. HUBERT ROBERT. 1733–1808. *France*

At the Hermit's

Oil on canvas. 64 × 48

79. JEAN HONORÉ FRAGONARD. 1732–1806. *France*
The Stolen Kiss

Oil on canvas. 45 × 55

80. CASPAR DAVID FRIEDRICH. 1774-1840. *Germany*
Nighttime in the Harbour (Sisters)

Oil on canvas. 74 X 52

81. ANTON RAFFAEL MENGS. 1728–1779. *Germany*

Self-Portrait

Oil on panel. 102 × 77

82. JEAN FRANÇOIS MILLET. 1814–1875. *France*

Peasant Women Carrying Faggots. *Ca.* 1858

Signed, bottom right: *J.F. Millet*

Oil on canvas 37.5 x 29.5cm

83. EUGÈNE DELACROIX. 1798–1863. *France*

Arab Saddling His Horse. 1855

Signed and dated, bottom right: *Eug. Delacroix 1855*
Oïl on canvas. 56 × 47

84. HORACE VERNET. 1789–1863. *France*

Self-Portrait. 1835

Inscribed and dated along the bottom edge: *Souvenir d'amitié d'Horace Vernet
au Comte de Ferzen. Roma 1835;* on the back: *Horace Vernet de ipse pinxit.
Roma*

Oil on canvas. 47 x 55

85. THÉODORE ROUSSEAU. 1812–1867. *France*

Marketplace in Normandy. 1830s

Signed, bottom right: *T. Rousseau*
Oil on panel. 29.5 × 38

86 CONSTANT TROYON 1810–1865 *France*

On the Way to Market. 1859

Signed and dated, bottom left: *C. Troyon 1859*
Oil on canvas. 260.5 × 211

87. CHARLES FRANÇOIS DAUBIGNY. 1817–1878.
France

The Banks of the Oise

Signed, bottom left: *Ch. Daubigny*
Oil on canvas. 25.5 × 41

88. CLAUDE OSCAR MONET.
1840–1926. *France*

Lady in the Garden (Sainte-Adresse).
1867

Signed, bottom left: *Claude Monet*
Oil on canvas. 80 × 99

89 PIERRE AUGUSTE RENOIR 1841–1919, *France*

Child with a Whip. 1885

Signed and dated, bottom right: *Renoir. 85*

Oil on canvas. 105 x 75

90. PIERRE AUGUSTE RENOIR. 1841–1919. *France*

Portrait of the Actress Jeanne Samary. 1878

Signed and dated, bottom left: *Renoir. 78*
Oil on canvas. 173 × 103

91. ALFRED SISLEY.
1839–1899. *France*

Villeneuve-la-Garenne on the Seine. 1872

Signed and dated, bottom left: *Sisley 1872*

Oil on canvas. 59 × 80.5

92 CAMILLE PISSARRO 1830–1903 *France*

Place du Théâtre-Français in Paris. 1898

Signed and dated, bottom right: *C. Pissarro. 98*
Oil on canvas. 65.5 × 81.5

93. VINCENT VAN GOGH. 1853–1890. *Holland*
The Bush

Signed, bottom left: *Vincent*
Oil on canvas. 72 × 92

94. VINCENT VAN GOGH. 1853–1890.
Holland

The Arena in Arles. 1888

Oil on canvas. 72 × 92

95. PAUL GAUGUIN. 1848–1903. *France*

Woman Holding Flowers. 1899

Inscribed, signed and dated bottom left: *TE AVAE NO MARIA*
Paul Gauguin 1899
Oil on canvas. 97 × 72

96. PAUL GAUGUIN. 1848–1903. *France*
Sunflowers. 1901

Signed and dated, bottom right: *Paul Gauguin 1901*
Oil on canvas. 72 × 91

97. HENRI MATISSE. 1869–1954. *France*

Bouquet (Vase with Two Handles). 1907

Signed, bottom right: *Henri Matisse*
Oil on canvas. 74 × 61

98. HENRI MATISSE. 1869–1954. *France*

Portrait of Madame Henri Matisse. 1913

Signed, bottom right: *Henri Matisse*
Oil on canvas. 145 × 97

99. MAURICE DENIS. 1870–1943. *France*

Spring Landscape with Figures (Sacred Grove). 1897

Monogrammed and dated, left, on the trunk of a tree: *MAUD 97.*
Monogrammed, bottom right, in the circle: *MAUD*
Oil on canvas. 157 × 179

100. MAURICE DE VLAMINCK. 1876–1958. *France*

View of a Town by the Lake. *Ca.* 1907

Signed, bottom left: *Vlaminck*
Oil on canvas. 80 × 99

101. PAUL CÉZANNE. 1839–1906.
France

Still Life with Curtain. *Ca.* 1899

Oil on canvas. 54.7 × 74

102. HENRI ROUSSEAU. 1844–1910. *France*

In a Tropical Forest. Struggle between Tiger and Bull

Signed, bottom left: *Henri Rousseau*
On the back: *Combat du tigre et du taureau. Reproduction de mon tableau exposé
au Salon des Indépendants 1908. Henri Rousseau*
Oil on canvas. 46 × 55

103. KEES VAN DONGEN. 1877–1968. *France*

The Red Dancer. *Ca.* 1907

Signed, bottom left: *Van Dongen*
Oil on canvas. 99 × 80

104. PABLO PICASSO. 1881–1973 *France*

Decanter and Tureens. 1908

Signed on the back, top left: *Picasso*
Oil on cardboard. 66 × 50.5

105. RENATO GUTTUSO. 1912–1987. *Italy*

Rocco and His Son. 1960

Signed, bottom right: *Guttuso*
Oil on canvas. 136 × 113

ЭРМИТАЖ.
ЗАПАДНОЕВРОПЕЙСКАЯ ЖИВОПИСЬ

Альбом (на английском языке)

Издательство „Аврора“. Ленинград. 1988
Изд. № 1605. (7-60)
Printed in Finland